Elmer's Tour

by former Governor
Elmer L. Andersen

foreword by Lori Sturdevant

photos by Richard Sennott

Copyright © Nodin Press 2005
All rights reserved. No part of this book may be reproduced in any form without the permission of Nodin Press except for review purposes.
Designed by John Toren
Nodin Press is a division of Micawber's, Inc.
530 N. Third Street, Suite 120
Minneapolis, MN 55401

NODIN PRESS

Introduction

Elmer L. Andersen was Minnesota's thirtieth governor, and much more. He achieved distinction as a businessman, journalist, legislator, higher education leader, dairy farmer, book collector, philanthropist and civic leader. At the time of his death in 2004, at age ninety-five, he was acclaimed as Minnesota's leading citizen.

Born in Chicago in 1909, Andersen was raised in Muskegon, Michigan, by an impoverished single mother. A job as a traveling salesman brought him to Minnesota in 1928. His decision to enroll in the University of Minnesota in 1929, and his connection that year with the love of his life, Eleanor Johnson of Minneapolis, cemented his bond with his adopted state.

Andersen went to work as a sales manager for a small St. Paul glue company in 1934; bought the company in 1941; and made H.B. Fuller Company a world leader in industrial adhesives and a model corporate citizen. He won a state Senate seat in 1949 and served nine productive years, leading state efforts in special education, welfare reform, higher education expansion, civil rights, metropolitan governance and natural resource protection.

He took those same policy themes into the governor's office in 1961, where he served as the last of Minnesota's two-year-term governors. A Republican, he lost his reelection bid in 1962 to DFLer Karl Rolvaag in what is remembered as one of the state's nastiest campaigns, and its narrowest outcome. Andersen was unseated by just ninety-one votes, after a four-month recount.

Defeat did not halt Andersen's work for civic good. After leaving the governorship he headed the Board of Regents of the University of Minnesota, the University Foundation, the Minnesota Historical Society, the Bush Foundation and the Lindbergh Foundation. He spearheaded efforts to establish Voyageurs National Park and enact a constitutional guarantee of fair taxation for taconite processors. He helped found the University of Minnesota Landscape Arboretum and its Andersen Library.

In 1975, he started a new career as an owner and publisher of community newspapers, and became an award-winning editorial writer. He became an author in 1997, when the first of his four books was published. His autobiography, *A Man's Reach*, won the Special Honor Award of the Minnesota Book Awards program in 2001.

Andersen donated more than 15,000 books to the University of Minnesota; his collection is housed in the archival library on the Twin Cities campus that bears his name.

Former Governor Andersen's health was flagging in June 2004 as he prepared to observe his ninety-fifth birthday. He had already filled the month's calendar with as many public events as stamina and prudence permitted. Yet when an opportunity arose to spend two afternoons roaming through his beloved Minnesota Capitol, he gladly seized it. Walking at his side those afternoons, watching him see fond details in his mind's eye (for his vision had largely failed him), I was sure that there was no place he would rather be.

The Capitol was much more than a building to Elmer. It was his workplace as a St. Paul state senator from 1949 to 1958 and as governor from 1961 to 1963. It was also his favorite manifestation of admirable aspects of the Minnesota character. In speeches, he often pointed to Cass Gilbert's masterpiece as an emblem of the optimism, confidence and pride of the sons and daughters of this state's founders. It celebrated their enterprise, revealed their devotion to democracy, and expressed their opinion that the people were as deserving of a palace as any prince. It showed that something beautiful and enduring can spring from an investment in the common good. It still can, Elmer would always say.

Elmer Andersen died on November 15, 2004. His remains returned to the Capitol one last time on November 18, to lie in state. I like to think that his spirit lingers there still, to inspire others who strive to serve Minnesota.

— Lori Sturdevant

Elmer's Tour …

One hundred years, the age of Minnesota's Capitol, is not long in the span of historical time. But it is long enough to test the character of a building. Minnesota's Capitol has scale, mass, and excellent design, but more than that, it has a wonderfully ethereal quality. It conveys the spirit of a people. It exudes the remarkable optimism of the generation that built it, less than a half-century after Minnesota became a state. Those pioneers wanted a center of government suitable for the state of distinction they were sure Minnesota would become. Their love of Minnesota, their dreams for its people, and their respect for its public servants are embodied in this Capitol, in ways grand and minute. The result is a hallowed place in which every Minnesotan can take pride.

    I was privileged to work in the Capitol, as a state senator and as governor, for thirteen years, and have been back often since then. I am grateful to the Capitol Centennial Commission for bringing me back once more, at age ninety-five, to describe for you my favorite Capitol places.

The Governor's Reception Room   1

The governor's reception room is a regular stop for school children who tour the Capitol. When I was governor, I had the rule that if I was nearby, I would speak to those students. I gave them a little message about the government and their place in it, and the opportunity that America affords. It's been gratifying in later years to meet grown-up people who say they still recall meeting me during their day at the Capitol in the fourth grade.

2 Table in Reception Room

This magnificent oval table befits the grandeur of this room, but it once bore an ornament that wasn't as fitting. When I was governor, the loon was designated as the state bird. Soon afterward, my friend Reuben Thoreen of Stillwater brought me a stuffed loon. He said, "I've been wanting to get rid of this darned thing, but my wife would never agree. But if I tell her that it's going to be in the reception room of the governor, she'll let me give it up." It was mangy and moth-eaten, but it was a loon. Somewhat reluctantly, I put it on this table.

Not long afterward, at the State Fair, I was approached by a girl who said, "I'm so happy that the state bird is the loon." I offered her the governor's office loon. She said, "I'd be thrilled. My parents would love it too." The loon was on its way to her house the next day. I had fulfilled my pact with Reuben Thoreen, and spared the reception room from a less-than-desirable element.

Hubert H. Humphrey Bust

There was a great deal to admire about Hubert Humphrey, and it's most fitting that he is remembered in the Capitol—even though his work as Minneapolis mayor, U.S. senator and the nation's vice president did not bring him to the chambers here. He had great talent as a speaker. I heard him speak to the St. Paul Rotary Club in 1944, while he was a young professor at Macalester College. He held the members spellbound. He had noble purpose and great talent; he loved people; and he worked hard to give people of all races equal opportunity. In his later years, he was imbued with ambition to become president, and he came close to achieving that goal in 1968.

Nicholas Coleman Bust

I liked Nicholas Coleman, who was DFL minority leader and then majority leader of the Senate in the 1970s. He was a genial, energetic leader who represented causes so well that people wanted to follow him.

I associate Coleman with Stanley Holmquist, my brother-in-law and the majority leader in the years when Coleman led the minority. These two men genuinely liked each other, and had common cause in improving the general welfare of the state. The worth of such relationships was proven in 1971, when there was a critical need for more funding for education. DFL Governor Wendell Anderson proposed shifting more responsibility for K-12 education to the state. That meant an increase in state taxes, and reform and reduction in local taxes. When Holmquist was satisfied that the DFL proposal was in the state's best interests, he swung a majority of the Senate to support it. It became known as the Minnesota Miracle—a wonderful example of how bipartisanship can function to advance the common good.

Stairway to the Senate

The stairway to the Senate is my favorite spot in the Capitol. Maybe that is because it leads to the Senate, for which I have such high regard. But every time I see this stairway's tremendous pillars, magnificent railing, outstanding materials and grand scale, I am confirmed in my opinion that the Capitol reaches its climax of beauty and design here.

Clara Ueland Plaque

Clara Ueland is one of only two women commemorated in the Capitol, and she certainly deserved the honor. She led the way for women's suffrage in Minnesota, and was an indefatigable worker in the cause. I've felt that there ought to be an annual observance at this plaque, to remind people that one dedicated person, with virtue and effort, can have great impact.

Sigurd Olson Bust

Sigurd Olson's life shows that one citizen, highly motivated and highly charged to serve, can do much. That possibility is greater in Minnesota than in many other places on earth. It deserves to be highlighted in our Capitol.

I first met Sigurd Olson when he came to the Legislature to testify in favor of a ban on airplane flights over the Boundary Waters Canoe Area. He was Minnesota's leading voice for wilderness protection, always controlled, eloquent, and sincere. We were allies, and became friends, during the long struggle to establish Voyageurs National Park.

Ingatius Donnelly Bust

Politician, populist, poet, scholar and more, Ignatius Donnelly is one of the most colorful characters in Minnesota history. He was elected the state's second lieutenant governor before age thirty, and was in and out of Congress and the Legislature for the next forty years. He died in 1901.

In the early 1950s, I noticed a print of the Donnelly home at a Historical Society exhibit. A little lady stood by it, absorbed in the image. I made bold to introduce myself, and ask the nature of her interest in the house. With a half-smile, she said, "I was Mrs. Donnelly." I gasped. More than fifty years had passed since his death! Then I remembered that late in life, Donnelly married his young secretary. Here she was, Marian Hanson Donnelly Woltman. I invited her to accompany me to the state Senate, to be introduced. The senators were astonished when I said, "I'd like to present the widow of Ignatius Donnelly."

Floyd B. Olson Portrait

Floyd B. Olson faced challenges as great as any governor in the history of the state. The populist movement swept him, a Farmer-Labor Party candidate, into office in 1930, as the Great Depression deepened. It was a terrible time. Olson told the people that the only way out of poverty is through investment in education. He proposed a new tax, on income, to be dedicated to education. The tax was enacted, and it had the desired effect.

Minnesota built one of the best systems of public education in the country, and prospered in the second half of the 20th century as a result. Olson is highly eligible to rank as the most outstanding governor in state history.

Harold Stassen Portrait

Harold Stassen was another of Minnesota's greatest governors. At age 31, as Dakota County attorney, he sought the governorship. He had to challenge the Republican Party's endorsed candidate in a primary to win. I was part of that election campaign in 1938. I knew Harold as a very high-minded person, studious, sober, and always working for the public interest.

He was called the Boy Wonder, for good reason. He brought a merit-based civil service system to state employment, and a constitutional ban on deficit spending to state finances. Already in 1940, he was both the keynote speaker at the Republican National Convention, and the floor manager for presidential candidate Wendell Wilkie. Stassen left the governorship in 1943 to join the Navy, and wound up as one of eight Americans chosen to draft the charter of the United Nations. He ran repeatedly for president in his later years, causing some people to poke fun at him. But he had a serious purpose: to draw attention to his ideas for a better nation.

Rudy and Lola Perpich Portrait

Often what is remembered most about governors and presidents is not what they accomplished in a material way, but what contribution they made to the spirit of the people. I think that applies to Rudy Perpich. He may have been the most lovable governor we ever had. He was full of enthusiasm, pride in his Iron Range roots, and love for this state. He adored his wife, Lola, and overcame controversy to include her in his portrait in the Capitol. I had a special relationship with Governor Perpich. When he was defeated the first time, in 1978, I happened to be in the Capitol the day after the election. I recalled how quiet things were when I lost the governorship. I checked, and he was in his office, all alone. We visited and commiserated for about an hour and a half. He never forgot that—and he did not give up on public service. When returned to office in 1983, he appointed me chairman of a commission to study higher education. He had big ideas, and worked hard to accomplish them.

Senate Chamber, Elmer's Desk

The Senate has such a beautiful chamber, rich with character and dignity. A constant inspiration to senators is the quote of Daniel Webster inscribed all around us, to the effect that people should try to do something worthy to be remembered. We members appreciated that feature.

My desk was in the front row, next to the aisle on the right side. That's a choice location. It had been Charles Orr's seat, which I inherited upon succeeding him after he died in office. It's a good spot for someone who likes to join in debate—so it suited me just fine.

Senate Retiring Room

The Senate is very jealous of this room. No non-senator is allowed in here, with very rare exception. This is a place where senators let their hair down and talk without benefit of listening news people. Many a deal were cooked here, away from the rival proponents of legislation. Co-authors for bills were sought out here. It was also a place for a senator to stretch out on the sofa and catch a catnap, away from public view. In my day, extreme partisanship was rare, and this was a convivial spot. I hope it still is.

House Chamber

Stepping into the House chamber reminds me of important occasions here. This is where governors deliver inaugural messages and state of the state messages. It's a fine place to give a speech. This is where Walter Mondale, as the 1984 Democratic presidential candidate, introduced his running mate, U.S. Representative Geraldine Ferraro. It was historic because, for the first time, a woman had been chosen to run for such a high office.

A prominent feature at the back of the House chamber is the large clock. It was the custom when I was a legislator to cover the clock when the constitutionally required hour for adjournment was approaching and bills were yet to be passed. They could go on for hours or even days like that. When I became governor, I announced that any bills passed after the actual deadline would be vetoed. That put an end to draping the clock.

View from the Press Alcove

There's always been tension between members of the Legislature and members of the press. When the Capitol was built, the members thought they had an opportunity to put a little space between themselves and the press. They provided that the press would observe House proceedings from the gallery. That lasted about one day. The press objected so strenuously that they were permitted in the alcoves at the back of the House chamber, where they've been ever since.

House Retiring Room

photo by Tom Olmscheid

I've often marveled at the proportions of this room. How beautifully related the length and width and height are to make it a perfect space. There was nothing overlooked in planning this Capitol building.

One happy occasion here was state Representative Willard Munger's birthday party. It may have been his eighty-fifth, in 1997. He was the state's longest-serving House member, serving with one two-year interruption from 1954 until 1999, when he died. He was Minnesota's leading voice for protection of our natural resources. A good crowd honored him—even though there was a snowstorm that day, so the band from Duluth that was supposed to perform didn't arrive. I have fond memories of sitting next to my good friend, former DFL Governor Orville Freeman that day. It may have been the last time we were together.

Ed Burdick Bust

The staff makes it easy for the body to function. I remember a faithful worker named Henry Southworth whose job it was to keep track of where every bill was, so that anybody interested in the status of a particular bill would ask Henry, and he would know. He was under the steps outside the Senate chamber.

Edward Burdick has been clerk of the House for more than forty years. He has great skill in keeping the bills in order, and in advising the speaker on the flow of business on the House floor.

Warren Burger Bust

U.S. Supreme Court Chief Justice Warren Burger was a Minnesotan whose involvement in Republican politics proved pivotal for his career. His work at the 1952 Republican National Convention helped secure the presidential nomination for Dwight Eisenhower. Eisenhower in turn put him in the U.S. attorney general's office, and then appointed him to the federal bench. President Nixon appointed him chief justice of the Supreme Court. It was a mighty trip for a young fellow who had his law training at night school at William Mitchell Law School.

Another bust should be here, honoring Minnesota's other Supreme Court justice, Harry Blackmun. He wrote one of the most important cases in court history, Roe v. Wade, protecting the personal rights of women to decide matters relating to their own bodies. His image is not in the Capitol because of the opposition of those who oppose abortion rights for women. When Burger and Blackmun were both on the high court, Minnesotans held two of the nine seats. I reasoned, that was about our fair share!

Supreme Court Chamber 19

The Supreme Court's offices moved to the Judicial Building in the 1990s, but the court's formal chamber remains here, as Cass Gilbert planned. That's as it should be. It deserves to be represented here in the Capitol. To convert this space to legislative use, as some have suggested, would be a sacrilege.

This chamber is somber, and the retiring room behind it is austere in comparison to the legislative retiring rooms. That's in keeping with the mission of the court. It's serious. It tells the rest of us what the law means, and it overrules the Legislature when it does something that violates the constitution. I've always thought that the judiciary is the most important of the three branches of government.

Capitol Approach

My predecessor in the Senate was Charles N. Orr, and he was majority leader. He was also instrumental in giving this grand building the setting it deserves. The Capitol building was surrounded for many years by a rundown residential area. Orr undertook negotiations with the city of St. Paul to buy land, move Wabasha Street, and secure the Capitol approach for the state. The result does him and this building great credit.